Original title:
Witty Walks in the Wild

Copyright © 2025 Creative Arts Management OÜ
All rights reserved.

Author: Rosalie Bradford
ISBN HARDBACK: 978-1-80567-208-1
ISBN PAPERBACK: 978-1-80567-507-5

Sprightly Steps and Stories

As I prance through the trees, so spry,
Chasing shadows that flicker and fly.
A squirrel scolds me with a cheeky grin,
While the wind whispers tales of where I've been.

I trip on a root, oh what a sight,
My laughter rings out, a joyful delight.
The leaves crackle under my dancing feet,
Nature's audience applauds, oh so sweet.

Giggles Through the Grass

In meadows brimming with daisies bright,
I stubble and tumble, quite the clumsy sight.
Bumblebees buzz with a playful tease,
While I dodge dandelions flying like bees.

Oh, watch me now, a leap and a roll,
Catching sunlight, oh what a goal!
The grass tickles as I scatter around,
With every giggle, joy knows no bound.

Cheery Chatters in the Canopy

High up where the chirping birds play,
I spy on the world in a silly way.
The branches sway, just like my mood,
As I tell secrets to the leaves, so rude.

Laughter echoes through the vibrant trees,
Join the chorus with the buzzing bees.
Swinging from vines, oh what a spree,
Nature's laughter, just you and me.

Quirky Quests of Exploration

Off on a quest, with a map upside down,
Hopping like a frog, in my explorer gown.
I chart the course by the clouds in the sky,
While a rabbit looks on, asking me why.

With each twist and turn, I spark a new game,
There's magic in mischief, this journey's so lame.
But every slip is a spin of a tale,
And with giggles aplenty, I shall never fail.

Gagging with the Gnarled Roots

In the forest, roots take hold,
A twisty tale, a sight so bold.
Tripping over nature's lace,
I laugh as earth delivers grace.

Beneath my feet, a gnome might dwell,
Whispering secrets; oh, what a swell!
They sneak up claiming, 'It's just a game,'
But who's to blame when they all look the same?

Punning by the Ponds

At the pond, the frogs do croak,
Each chirp a joke, like they're bespoke.
Splashing water with a leap,
While fish just roll their eyes in sleep.

A turtle grins, with clever wit,
Says, 'Slow and steady, that's my hit!'
While ducks quack in a feathered spree,
They all agree it's pure comedy.

Cheeky Channels of the Rivers

The river chuckles, flows with ease,
Dancing past the teasing trees.
With every bend, a splash of jest,
Where fish swim wearing their best vest.

A beaver builds with a wink and grin,
Crafting logs with a cheeky spin.
He shouts, 'This dam is quite the scene!'
As laughter echoes, oh so keen!

Jestful Jaunts Among the Trees

Among the trunks, a squirrel leaps,
With acorns tucked, while laughter peeps.
A woodpecker's knock, a rhythmic beat,
Turns the forest into a treat.

Mouse tales swirling, creatures prank,
Changing paths, with mischief rank.
Through leaves, we run, a merry chase,
In nature's playground, we find our place.

Roaming Through Revelry

In the woods where laughter blooms,
Trees wear hats that brighten rooms.
Squirrels dance in silly glee,
Chasing tails like it's a spree.

Bunny hops with rhythmic cheer,
Telling jokes for all to hear.
Leaves rustle with a giggly tease,
Nature chuckles in the breeze.

Nature's Playful Spirit

Frogs in hats sing silly tunes,
While ants host dance-offs in the dunes.
Sunbeams play hide and seek with shade,
As the meadows laugh, unafraid.

Wobbling worms with wiggly flair,
Have wrestling matches in midair.
The brook burbles nonsense all day,
Tickling stones in a playful way.

Side-Splitting Stretches

Stretching trees in funny poses,
Whispering secrets like bright roses.
Clouds dressed as clowns drift on by,
Painting giggles in the sky.

A picnic spread with food that sings,
Flying ants wearing tiny wings.
Grasshoppers hop on a trampoline,
Bouncing high like a comedy scene.

Chuckling at the Crickets

Crickets chirp in comic tones,
Tickling listeners in their bones.
Fireflies blink in rhythm bright,
Creating stars that twinkle at night.

A playful breeze begins to tease,
Shaking leaves with flickering ease.
The night wraps laughter in its cloak,
As joy and nature's humor evoke.

Nature's Laughing Path

A squirrel in shades, so cool and spry,
Dances on branches, reaching for the sky.
With laughter in leaves, the breeze gives a cheer,
Who knew the forest had such big dreams here?

A rabbit breaks out in a jittery jig,
While frogs croak a tune, making quite the gig.
The flowers all sway, in colors so bright,
As nature's own bands play from day into night.

Jests Amidst the Ferns

In the depths of the ferns, a pun is unspooled,
A fox tells a tale, while the raccoons are fooled.
With a wink and a grin, they share in the jest,
In a world full of giggles, they surely are blessed.

The mushrooms all clap when the beetles are bold,
Telling tall tales of adventures retold.
Each waving grass blade, a participant hums,
As echoes of laughter draw out all the chums.

Chuckles in the Underbrush

A hedgehog with socks, in a whimsical dash,
Tumbles through brambles, creating a splash.
The owls share a look, in bemused surprise,
As critters erupt into fits of arise.

The bumblebees buzz, with gossip on wings,
While the turtles debate who has the best bling.
In a tangle of joy, the bushes all sway,
As laughter rings out, brightening the day.

Amusing Footprints

Footprints in mud tell a story so grand,
Leading the way through a whimsical land.
With each silly step, the creatures delight,
In mischief and fun, from morning till night.

A moose with a hat prances through the tall grass,
While turtles in sandals are hoping to pass.
What wonders await on this comical spree?
In the game of the wild, it's clear—just be free!

Zany Zigzags Through the Woods

With acorns bouncing in the breeze,
Squirrels dance like they aim to please,
A raccoon hops on a log so slick,
Chasing shadows with a comic flick.

Pinecones tumble, rolling down,
A deer looks on, confused, wears a frown,
The rabbit laughs, a friend, quite bold,
Stashing snacks, a treasure to hold.

Sunlight flickers through the trees,
Tickling noses, stirring the bees,
A fox struts like he owns the place,
Invisible grin on his furry face.

So come, my friend, with merry feet,
Join the parade where nature meets,
With every turn, a giggle found,
In this wild dance, all joy abound.

Loquacious Labor of Love

The parrot squawks in playful jest,
Crafting stories, he's quite the best,
A turtle trips, but barely slows,
While ants tell tales, as the river flows.

There's mischief in the forest air,
A flurry of giggles, everywhere,
The owl hoots with a twinge of glee,
As frogs leap high, wild and free.

Breezes tickle the grass below,
Whispers of laughter, ebb and flow,
The wise old tree rolls its bark-eyes,
As critters plot their next surprise.

In the thicket, stories bloom,
Nature's theater, no time for gloom,
So gather 'round, let's share a line,
In this wild talk, we all intertwine.

Humor Among the Hills

In hilly heights where echoes play,
The goats wear hats, come join their fray.
With each step, laughter trails behind,
As squirrels debate what nuts they'll find.

A rabbit hops with style so bold,
While hedgehogs spin tales that never get old.
The breeze carries giggles through the trees,
As chipmunks dance in a jestful tease.

Flowers giggle as they sway,
Their petals whisper jokes all day.
As clouds parade with silly grins,
Nature's humor invites us in.

So roam these hills, let laughter soar,
Each grassy knoll holds tales galore.
With nature's jesters all around,
In humor's refuge, joy is found.

Lighthearted Labyrinths of Nature.

In tangled paths where shadows bend,
Each turn reveals a playful friend.
With mushrooms that giggle when you pass,
And streams that babble with a sass.

Frogs play leapfrog on lily pads,
While trees trade jokes, oh the laughs they had!
A hedgehog's wink, a bear's big grin,
In this forest, the fun won't thin.

A labyrinth crafted with whimsy and cheer,
Every twist and turn draws you near.
With bugs in bow ties who spin and twirl,
They invite you to join in a whirl.

So take a stroll, let nonsense bloom,
In every corner, dispel the gloom.
Nature's playground, where humor grows,
In lighthearted labyrinths, joy flows.

Strolling Through Satire's Grove

In a grove where sarcasm reigns,
Trees roll their eyes as humor gains.
With branches that snicker, and leaves that sway,
Nature's jesters brighten the day.

A crow caws jokes from high above,
While rabbits wear coats quite snugly proud.
In this woodland, laughter is common.
As critters create scenes that are never solemn.

A snake wears sunglasses, oh what a sight!
With turtles who race at their own delight.
Oh, the banter beneath the boughs,
Nature's humor knows just when to wow.

So wander through this playful scene,
With chuckles waiting around each green.
In satire's grove, the heart finds cheer,
With nature's antics, joy draws near.

Quips Beneath the Canopy

Beneath a canopy of vibrant hue,
The chatter of critters fills the view.
Squirrels crack wise as they gather their snacks,
While owls hoot riddles in leafy relax.

A parrot preaches in colorful tones,
While snickering raccoons raid picnics alone.
Flowers blush at the jokes they hear,
As bees buzz laughter, an annual cheer.

Beneath tall trees where shadows play,
Whimsical whispers lead the way.
With vines that tangle in playful fashion,
Nature's jesters stir up the passion.

So come and laugh under skies so wide,
In this thriving forest, let joy be your guide.
With quips that echo through each grove,
Amidst the creatures, life's humor roves.

Jovial Jaunts Through the Glade

In the glade where giggles bloom,
Squirrels dance, and mushrooms loom.
Bouncing bunnies twirl with glee,
Who knew nature could be so free?

Twisting paths with playful puns,
Every step a chance for fun.
A chatty crow with tales to share,
Makes even shadows laugh in air.

With twigs and leaves as quirky hats,
Chasing butterflies, avoiding cats.
In every nook, a joke awaits,
Nature's humor never abates.

As daylight flickers, night-time sings,
The frogs compete with banjo strings.
Under stars, we laugh and play,
In this wild wonder, joy's the way.

Smiles on the Summit

At the peak, where eagles soar,
We crack jokes, can't help but roar.
Clouds like cotton, fluffy and bright,
Nature joins in on our delight.

With every step, we share a laugh,
Finding joy in nature's path.
A tree with roots that dance and sway,
Competes with us in this merry play.

A lizard winks, it's quite absurd,
Chasing us with a teasing word.
The view is grand, yet here we stand,
Our hearts as light as grains of sand.

As sunset paints the world anew,
We giggle, sharing what we do.
For in this moment, joy's our kin,
On the summit, smiles have room to spin.

Riddles in the Rainforest

Amid the ferns, a riddle grows,
With laughing leaves and playful crows.
What has a bark but cannot bite?
An old tree's joke, it brings delight.

In shadows deep, we find a cheer,
Chattering monkeys draw us near.
Swinging vines with whispers sly,
A playful breeze makes time slip by.

Each droplet on the leaves does tease,
Tickling toes and dancing knees.
What runs but never walks a mile?
The river's giggle brings a smile.

In the labyrinth of greens so vast,
Every turn reveals a jestful cast.
Embrace the wild, let laughter reign,
In the forest's heart, joy's our gain.

Snickers by the Stream

By the stream where waters frolic,
We gather round, it feels symbolic.
A fish jumps high, and we all cheer,
Echoing laughter, so sincere.

Odd-shaped stones make funny faces,
Nature's artwork, in hidden places.
A turtle grins, it's quite a sight,
As dragonflies buzz in pure delight.

With every splash, a giggle flies,
As frogs croak back with silly cries.
What has a head but cannot think?
A rock's good joke makes us all wink.

With splashes loud and smiles wide,
We bask in joy, nowhere to hide.
By the stream, let laughter beam,
In nature's realm, we're a happy team.

Nature's Quirky Stroll

Amidst the trees, a squirrel prances,
Chasing shadows, taking chances.
A rabbit hops with flair and pride,
Dodging branches, eyes opened wide.

The chipmunk grins, a tiny thief,
Swiping snacks beyond belief.
A deer stands still, as if to pose,
While butterflies play peek-a-bo's.

The brook giggles, a bubbling tease,
Tickling stones with playful ease.
And every breeze has something to share,
Whispering jokes in the open air.

Nature's stage is set for fun,
Where laughter dances under the sun.
So grab your boots, let's take a stroll,
In this whimsical world, we find our soul.

Amusing Rambles Through the Thicket

Through leafy lanes where shadows play,
A raccoon rolls, what a clumsy display!
With sticky paws and a cheeky smile,
It leaves us chuckling for quite a while.

The flowers gossip, colors bright,
Telling tales from morning to night.
While ants march in a silly line,
Making plans for a picnic divine.

A hedgehog stumbles, bristly and round,
Creating laughter without making a sound.
And frogs croak songs with rhythmic glee,
As dragonflies flit, wild and free.

In this thicket of joy, we rollick and roam,
Finding humor in every little dome.
So step on soft leaves and enjoy the thrill,
In nature's embrace, our hearts are still.

Puns and Paths in the Underbrush

In the bush, a wise owl hoots,
Making puns that spark uproarious roots.
The fox, with a sly, mischievous grin,
Winks at the deer, asking, "Where you been?"

A path of mushrooms forms a quirky lane,
Where laughter bubbles like drops of rain.
The sunlight beams, a spotlight above,
Casting shadows that play and shove.

Beneath a tree, a tortoise scoffs,
Saying, "Slow and steady wins the scoffs!"
As squirrels bicker and chase for fun,
Life is a game when the day is done.

On these winding trails of whimsy and jest,
Every creature finds joy and is truly blessed.
So follow the puns and let spirits burst,
In nature's playground, laughter is first.

Laughter on the Trail

A parrot squawks, "I see you there!"
Joking about the hat you wear.
As we meander past bristles and blooms,
Nature's jests fill the air with tunes.

A clever lizard, sunning on a rock,
Yells, "Catch me if you can, tick-tock!"
While flowers sway, in garden attire,
Dancing around like a joyful choir.

The brook babbles secrets, splashing with glee,
Checking in with the ants: "What's new with thee?"
And every bird sings a tune so bright,
With puns that ignite the cool, starry night.

So onto the trail, where giggles abound,
With every step, new laughs we've found.
In nature's embrace, we share our wit,
Making memories that won't ever quit.

Amusements in the Arboretum

In the garden, squirrels play,
Chasing shadows, day by day.
Frogs are croaking silly tunes,
Dancing 'neath a chorus of moons.

A beetle wearing tiny shades,
Struts along the flower glades.
While bunnies stop to stretch and sigh,
Laughing at the passing sky.

A parrot squawks a joke so loud,
It makes the flowers burst with proud.
The trees nod in a leafy cheer,
As nature's jesters gather near.

With berries plump and frogs that sing,
Every moment's a zany fling.
Through every leaf, a playful breeze,
Brings hearty laughs 'neath shady trees.

Jovial Journeys

On the trail, a dog runs fast,
Chasing tails, his joy amassed.
A turtle races, slow and shy,
Dreams of crowns, oh, how he'd fly!

Birds gossip high on branches bold,
Sharing secrets from the old.
While rabbits hop and plot a scheme,
Of carrots sweet and sunshine's beam.

A fox in shades, so suave, so neat,
Dances on two paws, ain't that sweet?
While deer play hide and seek with glee,
This lively path is home to free.

Laughter echoes, a playful tune,
As each step stirs both sun and moon.
Nature's jesters, wild and wise,
Creating joy beneath the skies.

Mirth on the Mountain Trail

Up the hill, a goat does skip,
On a rocky path, it takes a trip.
It points to clouds, as if to say,
Join the fun! Come out and play!

A bear tries on a silly hat,
As birds all chuckle at the cat.
With every paw and feathered cheer,
The mountain's laughter draws us near.

A rabbit giggles, hopping high,
While ants march by with pies to try.
The sun peeks through with a wink and grin,
Nature's humor is where we begin.

As shadows stretch and daylight dims,
We share our joys, we sing our hymns.
With every twist and silly grin,
Mirthful moments, let's dive in!

Droll Detours

A wandering path, a twisty trail,
Where every footstep tells a tale.
A hedgehog dons a tiny coat,
As a ship-shaped leaf starts to float.

Chipmunks race to claim the prize,
A stash of nuts beneath the skies.
They stumble, fumble, tumble down,
With every roll, they paint a frown.

A crow caws loud, a comedian's tone,
Telling jokes with a swaggered moan.
While lizards bask on rocks, so wise,
Caught in laughter's mesmerizing guise.

With paths that twist like stories spun,
Each step reveals a new-found fun.
In nature's realm, with laughter's flair,
Every detour holds a playful air.

Jests of the Jungle

In the thicket, a monkey swings,
Telling tales as laughter rings.
His antics cause the birds to cheer,
While snakes just smile, not shedding a tear.

A parrot mimics all the jest,
As crickets chirp their loudest best.
They join the dance in leafy glades,
Creating cheer that never fades.

A jaguar winks with playful grace,
Challenging friends to a fun race.
In the jungle, every twist and turn,
Teaches all how much to learn.

Laughter bounces from tree to tree,
Echoing wild, unbridled glee.
With every step, come wise remarks,
Nature plays, igniting sparks.

Playful Paths Through the Pines

Among the pines, a hedgehog strolls,
Balancing acorns, playing roles.
A squirrel chuckles, gives a shout,
As pinecones roll, there's no doubt.

The chipmunks hide with tiny grins,
Planning pranks, and mischievous sins.
A raccoon dances, twirls around,
In this merry, forest bound.

As shadows grow and sun dips low,
The laughter of the forest flows.
Beneath the branches, tales unfold,
Of wise old owls and spirits bold.

In every step, a chuckle hides,
With playful friends, the fun abides.
Underneath the pines so grand,
Joyful moments at every hand.

Chuckles Beneath the Canopy

Beneath the branches, shadows play,
Where laughter hides from light of day.
An owl hoots out a funny rhyme,
While shy fawns giggle, lost in time.

A sly fox weaves through ferns so bright,
Turning twirls, bringing pure delight.
In the warm air, a breeze does sway,
Carrying chuckles far away.

With spirited leaps, the rabbits dart,
Joining the fun with a joyful heart.
Timing their hops with silly flair,
Filling the air with giggles rare.

Each critter shares a wild tale,
Of mishaps marked by laughter's trail.
In nature's arms, where joy's alive,
Each moment sings, it's how we thrive.

Mischievous Meanders and Moonlight

In the moonlight, shadows creep,
As creatures play, refusing sleep.
A raccoon steals a pie too sweet,
While fireflies flicker, moving fleet.

Through tangled vines, the mischief flows,
As giggles echo where no one knows.
A badger trips, falls with a thud,
Leaving footprints in the mud.

Above, the stars twinkle knowingly,
As nature unfolds in pure harmony.
With whispers soft, the night does hum,
Sharing secrets, laughter's drum.

In these meanders, joy runs free,
Where wild hearts meet under the tree.
Embracing the fun of a moonlit spree,
In this dance of nature, all is glee.

Capers in the Canopies

Crows are gossiping high above,
As squirrels dance with a nutty shove.
A parrot gives a loud mock cheer,
While the branches sway, the path is clear.

The lizard sports a tiny hat,
A bright pink feather, how about that?
The bumblebees buzz in delight,
As the sun sets, what's wrong feels right.

Frogs jump in rhythm, a croaky tune,
To the moon's glow, a silvery boon.
Treetops whisper secrets kind,
In this green world, joy is blind.

Laughter echoes through the leaves,
Playing tricks, this nature weaves.
Every shadow hides a jest,
In the woods, we're all blessed.

Amusing Asides on the Trail

A rabbit reading a dusty book,
Stops and gives you a wink and look.
With every hop, a tale to spin,
Of lettuce dreams and salad sin.

A turtle races, so slow, yet wise,
Wearing shades and a bright surprise.
He winks as he plods right along,
Belting out a quirky song.

The pathway twists with laughter bright,
Each rock a seat, a moonscape flight.
With every step, you meet a friend,
Nature's jest never seems to end.

The wind tells jokes in a playful breeze,
Tickling flowers beneath the trees.
With every turn, the fun unfurls,
In this wild play, the magic swirls.

Lively Legends of the Leaves

In the underbrush, a fox in a tie,
Swaps tales with a beetle flying by.
Frolicking stories, bubbling mirth,
In the dappled sunlight, all are birthed.

Leaves dance like they're at a ball,
As shadows play, they rise and fall.
A chipmunk juggles acorns with flair,
While the sting of laughter fills the air.

Whispers of owls spin yarns so grand,
As critters gather, a cozy band.
Every twist of the trail reveals,
A wild myth that laughter peels.

Creatures chuckle, the day's a fest,
With silly pranks, they never rest.
In forests deep, the fun's alive,
With every step, the spirits thrive.

Engaging Escapes

A porcupine dons a little crown,
Swaying side to side, he frowns.
His royal courtiers, a troop of ants,
Giggle as they join the dance.

The brook gurgles, making a tease,
While turtles try to catch the breeze.
Each ripple holds a chuckling spin,
As fish play tag, the game begins.

Grasshoppers leap, a quirky ballet,
Dressed in colors, oh what a display!
The sunbeams giggle, tickling toes,
As the garden fills with joyous prose.

In tangled vines, new jokes shall sprout,
Under the canopy, joy's about.
With every adventure that we take,
The wild's laughter is ours to make.

Frolics in the Forest

Twirling trees that wear a grin,
Squirrels dance, let the fun begin.
Mushrooms giggle, they're quite the sight,
Frogs croak jokes that last till night.

Bouncing leaves with every leap,
Nature's secrets we'll gladly keep.
The brook winks, splashing with cheer,
Chasing shadows, no need for fear.

The sun peeks through the leafy veil,
Whispering hints of a funny tale.
Rabbits chuckle, bunnies in a race,
In this joyful, wild, silly place.

So let's prance through this jolly glade,
Where every mishap's a grand parade.
In the heart of green, we find delight,
Amidst the laughter, all feels right.

Clever Paths Less Traveled

Taking the road where few dare to roam,
Finding mischief away from our home.
With tangleweed tickling toes in flight,
We chart a course with laughter and light.

The compass spins, it has a mind,
Leading us where the wacky's kind.
A tree stump waves; "Come sit for a bit!"
We toast with acorns, oh what a hit!

Invisibly roots that chuckle below,
Tickling feet, making us feel aglow.
Adventures bloom in snickers and quirks,
Silly encounters where playtime lurks.

We'll skip and skaddle, with joy on the map,
Invisible guides in this silly trap.
Each step's a giggle, with glee to unfold,
In paths less traveled, our stories are told.

Sarcasm in the Swaying Pines

Whispering pines with a sassy sway,
"Do you think you'll find your way?"
Branches chuckle in a breezy tone,
"Good luck, my friend, you're on your own!"

The path ahead looks a bit hazy,
With mushrooms saying, "Oh, isn't life crazy?"
Teasing shadows that dance with flair,
The forest mocks—"Life isn't fair!"

A raccoon rolls his eyes with a sigh,
"You called for help, but don't ask why."
With a wink and a nudge, he steals your snack,
"Watch your back; I don't cut you slack!"

Yet in the banter, we find our cheer,
In every roast, the laughter draws near.
Amidst the sass, we pitch our tents,
Finding joy in these clever laments.

Eclectic Expeditions

On a quest for fun, we zoom and dash,
Stumbling on stones, a merry clash.
The brook cries out, "Slow down, you fools!"
Every splash erupts with "Who needs rules?"

In the meadows where giggles grow,
We trip on daisies with a big "whoa!"
Butterflies flutter with sass on a breeze,
As if they're saying, "Take life with ease."

The trails twist left, oh now they turn right,
We follow our noses, not quite in sight.
With every misstep, we leap and bound,
In this bouncing joy, true fun is found.

So here's to the ramble and muddle we make,
To the quirky, the goofy, the laughs that we stake.
In every wild turn, we find our spree,
On eclectic journeys, forever carefree.

Jests in the Juniper Grove

In the grove, the squirrels joke,
Chasing tails, they're all bespoke.
A chipmunk chuckles, hides his stash,
While rabbits hop with a playful dash.

One tree limb bends with a graceful twist,
A bird on a branch says, 'Please don't miss!'
The wind whispers tales of mischief done,
As shadows play in the golden sun.

With every rustle, laughter blooms,
In the shade of soft, leafy rooms.
The pines lean in, they want to hear,
The tales of joy that fill the sphere.

So gather round, join in the jest,
Nature's humor, truly the best!
In the grove where giggles soar,
Laughter echoes forevermore.

Glee on Grassy Knolls

On soft hills, kids tumble free,
Rolling down with glee and glee.
A dog dashes, tongue out wide,
Chasing butterflies in joyous stride.

Picnic ants march, all in a line,
Stealing crumbs, oh so divine!
A butterfly lands, gives a wink,
While friends plot pranks over a drink.

A lone gopher peeks from his hole,
Rolling his eyes, one cunning soul.
He watches pranks, the laughter bursts,
In this place where joy immerses.

With kites that dance high in the breeze,
And giggles that carry through the trees.
On grassy knolls, hearts are light,
In this world where fun takes flight.

Quips by the Quagmire

By the swamp, the frogs proclaim,
'Lily pads are the way to fame!'
With croaks and leaps, they steal the show,
While dragonflies flit to and fro.

A turtle laughs with a cheeky grin,
'Slow and steady, I'll always win!'
But a raccoon shows up with a snack,
Saying, 'Get ready for a little hack!'

The mud squelches, a slippery stage,
As critters gather, filled with rage.
A heron winks and offers a jest,
Saying, 'Come on, the mud's the best!'

In the quagmire, the fun won't end,
Each muddy splash, a joyful blend.
With nature's quirks, laughter finds,
A welcome home for whimsical minds.

Revelry in the Ravine

In the ravine where shadows play,
The otters slide and shout hooray!
With splashes grand, they dance and dive,
In the water, feel so alive!

A raccoon sports a mask of mud,
'Fashion statement!' he says with a thud.
While a nearby fox, sly and spry,
Makes faces that could make you cry.

'What's the secret to your style?'
Asks a bird, staying for a while.
'It's easy! Just roll with the flow,'
Says the raccoon, putting on a show.

With every giggle, spirits rise,
In the ravine where fun never dies.
And as the sun dips low and bright,
Laughter echoes into the night.

Sassy Strolls Through Nature

A squirrel with a hat, oh what a sight,
Dancing on branches, full of delight.
Leaves whisper secrets, giggles unfold,
With every step, new stories are told.

A rabbit in shades, looking so cool,
Hopping by flowers, breaking the rule.
The pond reflects smiles, splashes of fun,
Nature's a jester, never outrun.

With each step forward, a chuckle is found,
As butterflies flutter, spinning around.
A game of tag with a vibrant blue jay,
In this playful world, who can delay?

The sunbeams wink down, lighting the way,
While grasshoppers leap, eager to play.
With every sassy step, joy takes a hold,
In nature's embrace, laughter is bold.

Laughter on the Leaves

Rustling leaves giggle, tell tales of the breeze,
A tickle from nature, puts minds at ease.
The mushrooms are blushing, so bright and so round,
In the midst of the forest, joy can be found.

A deer trying yoga, balanced on one hoof,
While butterflies tease, not far from the roof.
The sun mixing paints, with colors so bright,
Creating a canvas, pure laughter in sight.

The tufts of the grass sway, dance with the sun,
While ants hold a parade, having such fun.
Each giggle, each snicker, a gift from the earth,
Reminding us all of nature's mirth.

With flowers all dressed in their fanciest gold,
And bees buzzing secrets, jubilant and bold.
Laughter on leaves, where delight is the norm,
In this wild tapestry, chaos keeps warm.

Smirks in the Meadow

In a meadow of giggles, where wildflowers sway,
A fox with a grin, leads the dance of the day.
Each butterfly flutters with twists and with turns,
In the chorus of nature, the laughter returns.

A raccoon with mischief, eyes sparkling bright,
Steals berries away, what a dramatic sight!
The daisies are smirking, nodding with glee,
As crickets compose a light-hearted spree.

Set sail on a breeze, with sunlight as guide,
In this land full of smiles, happiness won't hide.
Clouds drift like popcorn, a show in the sky,
While the world shares a wink, as moments fly by.

The tall grass whispers, as secrets are spun,
In the heart of the meadow, joy weighs a ton.
Each step brings a chuckle, a smile—what a deal!
In nature's embrace, life's joys are so real.

Joking with the Junipers

With junipers jiving, the humor's been found,
Their playful green branches swaying around.
The sunbeams are teasing, casting long lines,
While shadows throw punches, delight in designs.

A porcupine ponders, "Should I wear this hat?"
As birds bust a move, they go flap-happy, pat!
The bushes can't stop laughing at all the fun,
In this playful realm, nature's never done.

A lizard in shades, lounging near a rock,
Winks and gives nods at the time on the clock.
The breeze plays a tune with an air full of zest,
As the world puts on smiles—it's nature's best jest.

Bouncing through twirls, like leaves in a spin,
Here's a wish for joy, let the good times begin!
With laughter in blossoms and jokes all around,
The junipers grin, here pure glee can be found.

Frolicsome Forest Forays

In the woods, a squirrel pranced,
Chasing shadows, it danced and chanced.
A bird called out with a cheeky squawk,
"Is that a fox or just a croc?"

The trees giggled as branches swayed,
While rabbits hopped in a joyful parade.
One tripped over a log, oh what a sight,
Laughter echoed, pure delight!

A deer, quite curious, peeked around,
Joined in the fun, no worries found.
With a leap and a kick, it showed off its flair,
"Who knew forest life could be so rare?"

As twilight fell, the critters met,
In a circle of fun, no regrets upset.
With stories and jokes, they shared the night,
For wild adventures made their hearts feel light.

Comical Conquests in the Clearing

In the clearing where grass grows tall,
A group of frogs had a bouncing ball.
They croaked and leaped with silly cheer,
A game of catch that drew them near.

A fly zipped by, causing a fuss,
"Get it, get it!" Oh, what a rush!
Amidst the splashes and froggy shouts,
Even the crickets joined the bouts.

A grasshopper cracked a rib-tickling joke,
While ants marched by, all orderly folk.
"Join us!" they cried, but still they'd scoff,
"Your slow little legs? Better hop off!"

With nimble jumps and playful pings,
The froggies forgot all sorts of things.
As the sun set low, their giggles soared,
In the clearing where joy is never ignored.

Jocular Journeys

Two turtles set out on a quest one day,
With backpacks and snacks, they planned their way.
"Let's travel fast!" one said with glee,
But a slow poke laughed, "Oh, not with me!"

With every step, new sights to see,
A butterfly waved, "Come chase with me!"
They stumbled upon a turtle dance,
From clumsiness, arrived a chance.

The duo twirled with style and grace,
"Is this speed? We're winning the race!"
A chipmunk cheered, "You've got the moves!"
As onlookers clapped, they started to groove.

Their journey turned into a festival bright,
With laughter and songs, the stars felt light.
No need for speed, they found the key,
Together they danced in wild jubilee!

Mirthful Marshlands

In the marsh, where the frogs like to sway,
A beaver arrived with plans to play.
"Let's build a club for all to meet!"
He claimed with a grin, "Come join my seat!"

The turtles rolled in, with shells like art,
And painted the pond, a marvel to start.
While dragonflies buzzed with curious ease,
Joking, they teased, "Mind the soggy leaves!"

With reeds as the walls and lilies for chairs,
The marsh threw a bash with laughter to spare.
Ducklings wiggled, showing their flair,
"Jump into the fun! Don't you dare despair!"

As night enfolded, the creatures were bright,
Swapping tales of daring with pure delight.
In murky waters, they found their bliss,
Mirth in the marsh, impossible to miss!

Whimsy in the Wilderness

In the forest, squirrels debate,
Who can leap and who can skate.
A rabbit laughs at the owl's stare,
Wings flapping wildly, feathers in the air.

A fox tries to dance, but trips on a root,
While the deer giggles, it's quite a hoot.
The bushes buzz with gossip and jest,
As bees break dance, they're simply the best.

With mushrooms wearing hats of green,
And chipmunks hosting a dance routine.
The ferns raise their fronds, cheering on the show,
Nature's comedy, it's all for the glow.

Under the stars, the laughter ignite,
As fireflies twinkle, a glowing delight.
With the moon as a spotlight, the night comes alive,
In the whimsy of woods, everyone thrives.

Hilarity in the Hollow

Down in the hollow, where giggles abound,
A turtle sings operas, quite a strange sound.
The hedgehogs roll 'round, in a clumsy ballet,
While frogs croak the chorus, in their own quirky way.

A raccoon with style, wearing a crown,
Juggles acorns and leaves, but tumbles down.
The critters all cheer, it's quite the parade,
Under leafy umbrellas, in shade, they're displayed.

The sun winks down, tickling the breeze,
As squirrels play poker behind the tall trees.
With acorn bets, and nutty delights,
Their laughter echoes through long, playful nights.

And when the dusk falls, the laughter won't fade,
The moon takes the stage, a bright serenade.
From creatures all around, a jovial spree,
In the hollow of hilarity, wild and carefree.

Folly and Footprints

Footprints of folly dance in the dirt,
As the goose wears a hat, looking quite pert.
A squirrel on stilts, it sways to the sound,
Of crickets composing their symphonic round.

The hedgehog recounts tales of grand schemes,
Adventuring far, fueled by wild dreams.
A group of bright mushrooms joins in the fun,
Flickering softly, their laughter begun.

A game of hide and seek, the hares take to flight,
While the owl plays the judge in the fading light.
The paths twist and turn, a riotous mess,
Of folly and footprints, with joy to express.

And as day turns to night, with a shimmering glow,
The creatures unite for a wild comedy show.
In this realm of the playful, under stars' bright streams,
The folly of nature is woven in dreams.

Banter on the Breeze

The breeze carries giggles from Tom and his mates,
As they tease the old owl about all of his dates.
The wind whispers secrets to trees all around,
While rabbits play cards on the soft, leafy ground.

A butterfly flutters, gossip in her wings,
Talking of frogs as they plan their spring flings.
The daisies lean in, eager to hear,
While a fox plays the piano, spreading good cheer.

Banter flows freely, it tickles the air,
As turtles discuss the best ways to share.
The acorns exchanged yield laughter and glee,
In this playful domain, life's a comedy spree.

With each gust of wind, tales twist and collide,
The creatures unite, their humor their guide.
In the dance of the wild, where joy comes in waves,
Banter on the breeze is what nature craves.

Antics Among the Alder

A squirrel wears a tiny hat,
He chats with birds and laughs a lot.
The trees, they giggle, swaying fast,
As nature plays, a joyful blast.

The rabbit hops with twinkling eyes,
Chasing butterflies in bright blue skies.
A dance of leaves, a rustle here,
The forest chuckles, full of cheer.

A fox with pranks hides in the brambles,
He springs surprises, oh how he scrambles!
The ants parade in silly rows,
Telling tales as the laughter flows.

Through twigs and thickets, tittering tones,
Each creature's antics serve as homes.
With every step in this wood so grand,
The humor wraps us, hand in hand.

Cheerful Treks Through the Thorns

Beneath bright blooms, the hedgehogs sing,
Waddling 'round in a jolly ring.
Rose bushes poke, but they don't mind,
In every prickle, a giggle's lined.

The bees hum tunes of funny fables,
As bugs dance on the picnic tables.
A greedy snail, he slides on by,
Longing for crumbs, oh my, oh my!

With clumsy feet, the mole does trot,
Stumbling over stones, he's quite the plot.
The thorns might scratch, but hearts are light,
In every scratch, a comic sight.

Colors clash in the sunny patch,
Where laughter lives with a cheerful catch.
A winding path, with stories to glean,
Each thistle a grin, each turn a scene.

Stories of the Wildwood

In the wildwood, tales abound,
The owls whisper secrets around.
A rabbit tells of moonlit feasts,
With dancing bugs and humming beasts.

A deer recounts a funny chase,
With a squirrel who swore he'd won the race.
Beneath the stars, they laugh and play,
Each tale more wild than the last hooray.

Night birds cackle, a raucous crew,
As fireflies light up stories anew.
With every flicker, the laughter grows,
In wooded realms, glee surely flows.

Across the glen, wise trees confide,
In every knock, they prance with pride.
The wildwood's heart, a comic stage,
Where nature's humor sparks the page.

Merriment in the Meadow

Fluffy sheep with woolly curls,
Play leapfrog with the dancing swirls.
The daisies sway, they join in fun,
Under the bright and shining sun.

A playful calf, he skips along,
Chasing shadows, a joyous song.
The crickets chirp their silly tunes,
While butterflies flutter like wild balloons.

The winds carry laughter, soft and free,
As nature's jesters perform with glee.
A picnic spread and ants parade,
Each little morsel, a grand escapade.

Above the blooms, a sky of blue,
With every hop, more laughs accrue.
In this meadow, joy clearly shows,
Where merriment in each heart glows.

Joyful Jaunts

In the woods where laughter rings,
Squirrels dance and robins sing.
Bouncing berries on a stick,
Nature's humor – oh, so quick!

Trees wear hats made of leaves,
While bees make honey, bold and thieves.
Every corner turns a grin,
With playful spirits tucked within.

Frogs in boots jump high and low,
Chasing shadows, putting on a show.
Mushrooms giggle, twirling round,
As sunshine laughs upon the ground.

With each step, a chuckle flows,
In every rustle, laughter grows.
Joyful jaunts, a clever scene,
In this forest, we're all keen!

Guffaws on Green Trails

On the path where daisies grow,
Wiggly worms put on a show.
Bunny hops with style and grace,
Sporting a smile, a furry face.

Butterflies wear fancy hats,
As ants march past like tiny brats.
Flowers gossip in the breeze,
Sharing secrets, laughing with ease.

Squirrels tease with acorn throws,
While daisies twirl in leafy prose.
Laughter echoes, bright and clear,
In this wild, there's much to cheer!

Every stumble starts a giggle,
Makes each trek a playful wiggle.
Guffaws on trails where jesters thrive,
In every step, we come alive!

Snickers Along the Stream

Down by the banks where waters sigh,
Fish leap up, then wink goodbye.
Rocks with faces, old and wise,
Whisper jokes beneath blue skies.

Tiny toes dip in the flow,
As willows wave with a subtle glow.
A turtle grins, takes his time,
Each slow move a perfect rhyme.

In the reeds, the frogs align,
To croak out notes, a funny line.
Dragonflies glide, twirling about,
As the stream giggles, there's no doubt.

With each ripple, a chorus sings,
Nature's laughter, full of springs.
Snickers in water, life's sweet tease,
In this realm, we find our ease!

Playful Paces

Through the fields where daisies peep,
Jumping jacks make sheep awake from sleep.
Breezes play tag; clouds drift and sigh,
As kids chase shadows and butterflies.

The hills roll over, giggling fast,
Rolling down, none can outlast.
With muddy boots and smiles so wide,
Laughter floats like the moonlit tide.

Puppies chase their tails so spry,
While giggles soar up to the sky.
Each playful skip, a jolly cheer,
As nature dances, drawing near.

With each step, fresh stories brew,
In wilds alive, where fun is true.
Playful paces, a joyful chase,
In this blissful, happy place!

Rambles in Rhyme

A squirrel with shades, oh what a sight,
Dancing on branches, feeling just right.
The wind can't help but laugh at his moves,
Nature's own jester, nothing to prove.

A chipmunk sings, though tone is a mess,
While beetles applaud, in tiny finesse.
With every mishap, a giggle ensues,
They're all just here for some silly news.

Trees sway along, in rhythm with glee,
As they share the punchline, just wait and see.
An owl adds wisdom, tipped with a snort,
In this leafy circus, all humans are sport.

So gather the friends, the laughter, don't cease,
In this merry wood, find your inner peace.
With playful vibes, and gags that repeat,
Life's just a jest, come join the heartbeat.

Humor in the Haze

Through morning mist, a rabbit hops light,
His ears flop around, what a goofy sight.
He tries to be stealthy, a comical feat,
But his bouncy little dance just can't be discreet.

A badger joins in, with a snicker and grin,
Stumbling and tumbling, he spins round and spins.
The fog laughs along, with each silly turn,
In this playful show, there's much to discern.

The sun starts to peek, through clouds that do tease,
A chorus of critters sings out with unease.
But laughter erupts when the shadows do dare,
To leap from their hiding, springing everywhere.

So follow the trail where the silly things roam,
Where joy is the compass leading us home.
Adventures await in each rustle and buzz,
In the haze of humor, oh, just because!

Whimsical Wilderness Journeys

A fox in a bowtie, how dapper he looks,
Writing his memoirs in old storybooks.
He sips on some nectar, among daisies bright,
While a crow takes a selfie, it's quite the sight!

Twisting through brambles, a snake tells a tale,
Of adventures so wild, never a fail.
His laughter is bubbly, like soda it rolls,
In this jungle gym, joy feeds the souls.

With every new path, a riddle unfolds,
The trees clap their hands as the fun never holds.
A bear holds the drum, with a hairy display,
Together they jam, in a furry ballet.

So off on your journey, leave troubles behind,
In whimsical settings, true magic you'll find.
With smiles that sparkle, and stories that glide,
Let laughter be your very best guide.

Banter Between the Boughs

Two trees whisper secrets, their branches entwined,
Sharing sweet laughter, in breezes combined.
A woodpecker chimes in with rhythmic insists,
While ants crack a joke, they can't help but gist.

A chipmunk debates which acorn is best,
While a raccoon nearby looks utterly stressed.
Tales of the night, filled with snacks and delight,
Are shared with such vigor, till the dawn's first light.

With shadows that dance on the forest's warm floor,
Mice gather for gossip, their voices can soar.
"Did you hear about Sally? She found the last nut!"
"Oh no," squeaks a friend, "let's give her a cut!"

So wander through pathways where chitchat ignites,
In this world of folly, enjoy all the sights.
Nature is spirited, in laughter we bond,
A playful communion, of joy we respond.

Sassy Strides

Through the woods we prance with glee,
Each twist and turn, a jubilee.
We trip on roots, then laugh aloud,
Our legs are limber, our spirits proud.

A squirrel darts by, a cheeky tease,
With acorn in paw, it aims to please.
We mimic their dance, with flair and cheer,
In nature's theater, we're without fear.

The brook sings softly, a jokester's tune,
Bubbling laughter beneath the moon.
We splash and we play, like children bold,
In the heart of the wild, adventures unfold.

Each step a giggle, with friends so dear,
Chasing the sunlight, our laughs sincere.
Through thickets and trails, our spirits high,
With sassy strides, we dance through the sky.

Pranks of the Path

On the path of the green and gold,
We plot some mischief, uncontrolled.
A stick like a snake, we toss with glee,
Watch out for jumps—who's next? Not me!

A friendly nudge, a gentle shove,
Into a bush, my oh my, love!
With twigs in hair, we laugh and shout,
Those pesky brambles, can't do without!

Blown dandelions float like dreams,
We chase them down in wild, wild schemes.
"Oh, look at that!" with snickers abound,
The shoes get muddy, laughter profound.

Through the laughter, the pranks unfold,
With each new trick, a memory bold.
In the woods, our spirits thrive,
As pranksters of the path, we come alive!

Hearty Humor in the Hills

In the hills where the breezes tease,
We share a toast with cups of leaves.
With berries plucked, we play a game,
Who can make faces? All the same!

The shadow of clouds plays chase with the sun,
We giggle and stumble, our race just begun.
Rolling downhill, the laughter flows,
Like playful pups, just fooling around, who knows?

With every misstep, hilarity reigns,
Tripping on rocks, losing our brains!
We toss out quips like glittering rays,
In the hills, every laugh surely stays.

So let the winds carry our cheer,
Each hearty chuckle is what we hold dear.
For nature's our stage, and we play it right,
In the hills where the humor is bright.

Jests of the Journey

With backpacks slung and spirits high,
We march along, under the sprawling sky.
Each step a jest, a tale unfolds,
Our laughter weaves the journey it holds.

"Look at that fence!" a friend's quick claim,
A wild goat stands, but it's all just a game.
We mimic its bleats, in silly delight,
As onlookers ponder if we're all right.

The sun dips low, casting goofy shapes,
We dance like shadows, turning into apes.
With whimsical hops, we frolic and play,
At every corner, smiles on display.

Jests of the journey, we carry within,
In every laugh, a joyful spin.
With friends at our side, and trails that unfold,
The stories we share are worth more than gold.

Wisecracks and Wildflowers

In fields of blooms, where laughter grows,
A bee buzzed by with a pun that flows.
"Why do flowers always seem so bright?"
"They got a sunny disposition, alright!"

The daisies danced, their jokes were punny,
Telling tales of storms and honey.
"What did the tulip say to the rose?"
"Stop smelling like you're in the nose!"

Every petal held a playful jest,
As critters joined in, they felt so blessed.
"Why did the garden stop its chatter?"
"Its soil was tired of all the clatter!"

With nature's giggles, the day was done,
As sunset whispered, "We had our fun!"
"Don't forget to bring your joy tomorrow!"
"Or else these wild blooms will be full of sorrow!"

Jolly Jaunts Through the Jungle

Among the trees, where shadows creep,
A monkey swung with a joke so deep.
"Why did the lion cross the track?"
"To show the zebra who's got the knack!"

The parrots cawed, with colors bright,
Their chatter echoed from left to right.
"Why don't snakes ever get lost, you see?"
"Because they follow their own slippery glee!"

On vines we swung, like no care at all,
In this leafy land, we laughed and sprawled.
"What did the jaguar say to the ant?"
"You're small but mighty, that's a sure chant!"

In this jungle realm, where humor thrived,
The spirit of fun always survived.
"Let's stroll again when the sun's on high!"
"I'll bet there's more jokes under the sky!"

Laughing Leaves

The rustling leaves began to tease,
Whispering laughs with the gentlest breeze.
"Why do trees love to gossip so?"
"Because they share roots, like it's all a show!"

A squirrel chattered, with antics grand,
Juggling acorns, his furry band.
"What's a tree's favorite kind of music?"
"Anything with a good root, it's just acoustic!"

The branches wiggled, with joy combined,
As green-fingered friends left worries behind.
"Why did the pine needle start to sing?"
"Because it wanted to be the next big thing!"

In nature's stage, the leaves would play,
With giggles and joy that brightened the day.
"Don't forget to laugh in the sun's warm glow,
Or else the forest might just steal the show!"

Whimsy on the Wilderness Way

On trails untamed, where mischief stirs,
A rabbit pranced, strutting its furs.
"Why don't we ever play hide and seek?"
"Because I'll hop away, in less than a week!"

The hedgehogs chuckled, all clumped in a row,
"What's the best way to share a slow show?"
"With lots of hugs and maybe a snack!"
"But be careful, or your picker won't come back!"

Around the bend, where the flowers peek,
A cow exclaimed, "Well, this is unique!"
"Why don't we hear cows telling tales?"
"Because their jokes always get stuck in theirails!"

As twilight fell, the fun did not cease,
In the heart of the wild, we found our peace.
"Let's roam again with a giggle and grin,
For in the wilderness, the laughter won't dim!"

Bantering with the Breeze

The wind whispers jokes, oh so sly,
Leaves chuckle back, as they flutter by.
Sunbeams giggle, tickling the trees,
Nature's laughter dances with ease.

A squirrel jests with a nut in tow,
While wise old owls roll their eyes, you know.
The brook gurgles with a cheeky tone,
Bantering softly, never alone.

Clouds trade quips in a fluffy white gown,
While shadows shift, never wearing a frown.
Laughter echoes through the open space,
A spirit of joy found in this place.

So join the fun, let your heart take flight,
Where nature shares giggles morning to night.
In the wild, each step is a playful tease,
Bantering sweetly with the teasing breeze.

Puns Along the Pathway

On the trail, a punster's delight,
With every step, a new word takes flight.
Trees bark jokes, branches extend,
Nature's wit flows without an end.

A rabbit hops in with ears set high,
Says, "I'm on a roll, but don't ask why!"
The flowers giggle, petals all a-twitch,
"Stop and smell us, it's quite the niche!"

A rustling bush offers a sly retort,
"Why did the chicken leave? It's out for sport!"
With every turn, a whimsical twist,
Laugh along as the path can't be missed.

So if you stumble, just chuckle and play,
For puns escape in a lively display.
With mirth and mirages lighting the way,
Every step taken makes the heart sway.

Light-Hearted Escapades

With every stride, a giggle we seek,
Through fields of laughter, so funny, so cheek.
Butterflies flutter, dressed in a grin,
Chasing the sun, they spin and they kin.

A playful breeze gives a tug on my shirt,
"Catch me if you can!" it flirts from the dirt.
Grasshoppers jump, making leaps so grand,
As I join in their dance, hand in hand.

The hills whisper secrets, all bubbly and bright,
Turning each moment into pure delight.
With every twist, a tummy right aches,
In wild escapades, a laughter awakes.

So run through the wild, with joy in your chest,
Light-hearted adventures surely feel best.
Let nature's antics be your wild guide,
With smiles and puns, let the fun abide.

Skits in the Scenic Shadows

In the quiet nooks, shadows play tricks,
They dance and they jive, with laughter in flicks.
A deer on the side cracks a joke so sly,
"Why do we prance? To reach for the sky!"

The sun peeks in, giggling through the leaves,
While squirrels perform, in acorn reprieves.
A playful bear does an impromptu ballet,
As we clap for joy at this furry cabaret.

A raccoon stumbles, all bandit-like fun,
"Just here for the snacks, not a single pun!"
With echoes of laughter draping the span,
These skits in the wild, scripted by a plan.

So linger a moment, let shadows entice,
In nature's theater, everything's nice.
From critters to whispers, a comical show,
Step in for a scene, let the jesting flow.

Chuckling at the Clouds

On fluffy peaks, we laugh and play,
The sky's a canvas, bright and gray.
A raindrop lands, tugs at my nose,
I dance around, as laughter flows.

The sun peeks out with a sneaky grin,
While shadows stretch, and giggles spin.
A cloud's lost fluff floats by my ear,
Whispering jokes only I can hear.

With every breeze, there's chuckles anew,
I chase silly thoughts like a kid would do.
A playful gust gives my hat a toss,
And suddenly, I feel like a boss!

So here we are, beneath the skies,
Where whimsy sprinkles, and laughter flies.
In every puffy shape, I find a joke,
Together we ponder and happily poke.

Breezy Banter Among Branches

Among the leaves, a squirrel prattles,
While birds debate in chirpy rattles.
A twig snaps loud, a comedy scene,
The trees crack jokes, if you know what I mean.

A breeze winks by, tickles my ear,
I laugh with the wind; it's all good cheer.
The branches sway, as if they sway,
To the rhythm of nature's bright cabaret.

A bumblebee buzzes, a clumsy dance,
Upside down in a flower's expanse.
He stumbles and tumbles, and I can't help but grin,
Nature's own jester, with a fluffy chin!

So here we gather, where giggles ignite,
With trees as our comrades, from morn until night.
In playful chatter, we share our tale,
Of breezy banter that'll never pale.

Frivolity Under the Firs

Under tall pines, the shadows play,
Where giggles echo and children sway.
A pinecone drops with a plump little thud,
Nature's own slapstick, a real good bud!

The crickets join in; they chirp on cue,
Making a symphony just for you.
A squirrel in shades struts down the line,
Wearing mischief like it's fashion divine.

I trip on a root and fall with a thump,
But laughter's the sound that replaces the slump.
The firs sway gently, in musical grace,
As they watch my antics with a verdant face.

So come join the fun, beneath leafy skies,
Where silliness bubbles and laughter flies.
In every moment, a jest we release,
Finding joy in our folly, and pure, sweet peace.

Lighthearted Lark in the Wilderness

In the wild, where tickles roam free,
Every twig is a beam of glee.
I leap over logs, a clumsy dance,
With laughter twirling, it's pure romance.

A playful deer gives me a stare,
As if to say, 'Is that your best flair?'
I grin at the shrubs, they giggle back,
In this silly world, there's nothing we lack.

A stream gurgles with secrets galore,
It splashes funny tales from the forest floor.
As flowers nod, they join in the jest,
Nature's own show, simply the best!

With every step, a new chuckle awaits,
Among the wild things, where laughter creates.
So let's dance through the woods, with hearts full and light,
In this whimsical realm, everything feels right.

Joking with the Junipers

In juniper's shade, a squirrel did jest,
He challenged a crow, 'Let's see who's the best!'
With acorns as bombs, they mocked the tall pine,
Laughter erupted, oh, how they did shine!

A rabbit chimed in with a joke so absurd,
'The grass is much greener, have you heard the word?'
The owls rolled their eyes, trying hard not to blink,
While raccoons all gathered, sharing nibbles and drink.

'The breeze is a comedian,' chuckled the breeze,
'Telling tall tales through the rustling leaves!'
The shadows all danced to the rhythm of cheer,
In nature's own theater, laughter is clear!

So gather your friends, take a stroll under trees,
There's humor to find if you're willing to tease!
In juniper's realm, the play never ends,
Just follow the giggles where wild whimsy bends!

Fables of the Forest

Among the tall fables where the tall tales reside,
A fox with a mustache pranced with such pride.
He offered a hare some old socks for a prize,
'They smell of adventure!' he said with sly eyes.

A turtle strolled by, with a wink and a grin,
'Fast doesn't mean fun, let the slow dance begin!'
With turtles and hares joining round in a circle,
The forest burst forth with their laughter, a whirlpool!

As leaves floated down, like confetti in flight,
A badger recited his jokes into night.
Each pun made them howl, sent trees bending low,
In fables enchanted, where laughter would flow.

In this leafy arena of mirth and delight,
The stories kept spinning from morning to night.
Next time you wander, let giggles be heard,
In the heart of the wild, let joy be preferred!

Satire Among the Shrubs

A shrub with a quip made a strong debut,
'The more you water me, the less I can chew!'
With thorns for a punchline, it pricked at the air,
Leading chuckles and snickers from passerby stare.

The daisies rolled eyes, playing preacher and sage,
'This bloom is a blunder, throw him off the stage!'
Yet the lilacs all giggled, they loved the whole scene,
A satire of nature, both silly and keen.

The wind brought a jest from a far away tree,
'I've seen all your antics, just wait! You'll agree!'
As branches and leaves joined the chorus of mirth,
A festival bloomed, celebrating the earth.

So if you find shrubs, throwing shade just for fun,
Remember their humor shines bright like the sun.
In nature's delight, let laughter take root,
For shrubs have their wisdom, in each silly loot!

Guffaws and Gaiters

In gaiters now donned, our feet led the way,
Through puddles and laughter, we danced on our play.
With each slip and slide, we'd snicker and squeal,
While nature looked on, enjoying the reel!

A moose passed by wearing boots that were bright,
'They're stylish, you know! For a forest fashion fight!'
He strutted and pranced, a deer joined his spree,
'Is that plaid with polka dots? Oh, do let me see!'

The trees shook with laughter as we shared all our woes,
Chasing our shadows as the wild river flows.
With puddle-filled giggles and gaiters galore,
Every step sparked joy, leaving hearts wanting more!

So lace up your shoes as we wander about,
See where the footpath may lead, without doubt.
In this cheerful parade, let merriment reign,
For laughs in the wild surely give pleasure immense!

www.ingramcontent.com/pod-product-compliance
Lightning Source LLC
Chambersburg PA
CBHW051641160426
43209CB00004B/747